No Stranger

to

The Truth

Clive Pearson Evans

LLYFRAU
CAMBRIA

Published in the United Kingdom in 2015 by
Cambria Books, Wales, United Kingdom

Acknowledgement

I wish to thank Rob Haines for supplying the cover photograph and Tony Wood for encouraging me to pursue this publication and who was instrumental in seeing it through.

The Poems

Return to the Labyrinth

Back here from yesterday they come
To where the home is still
Perhaps one memory to find
That time forgot to kill.

One friend, one unique place
One never changing street
That last undying rose
Petalled flower complete.

Now as they wander through the
Labyrinths of yesterday
They will never find the things
Years have taken on the way.

The search for freedom led them down the route they risked.
To stay or not to stay was the question that they asked.
To live with what they knew and loved, or travel far to find
That what they stood to gain was what they left behind.

Final Notice

Composed upon looking over the wall at the sorry state of Cefn Coed Cemetery.

Within the walls the toppled gravestones lay
A playground now where truant kids hold sway.

Above a grave, an earthbound angel stands
A broken harp upheld in outstretched hands.

Here left to rest a husband, a wife
With pink plastic flowers, the only
Testament to a once cherished life.

Stones that once marked out our beloved dead
Lay broken now, a hazard sign instead
Highlights not their earthly role
But warns us to avoid the hole.

Here and there lie shallow graves
Unearthed to tell the story
Of council skulduggery
Not to celebrate death's glory.

For this neglect, this disrespect
For now we rail, recriminate
Against them but just as the sun
On distant hills begins to set
We will eventually forget.

Our memories will falter
Just as the gravestones shatter,
Two generations down the line
To them what will it matter.

The Merthyr Whale

The day the whale came to Merthyr
We all went down for a look.
It was up on a lorry by the old iron bridge
And they never caught that on a hook.

They was charging a shilling to see it.
All us kids, we thought it was grand.
Took us behind an old tarpaulin
And give us a stamp on the hand.

The man that found it was called Jonah.
They said he was a bit of a wag.
He sat on a stool counting money
While pulling on the butt of a fag.

He told us how first he had found it
One night on a beach in the rain.
And with a keen eye for business,
He swore, 'Whale, you'll not swim again.'

Strolling down to the beach at Barry,
Councillors reconnoitred the scene.
Jonah they found was no longer around
And the whale was not there but had been.

The councillors saw red but it has to be said
Jonah, the culprit, was sound asleep in his bed
With the whale bundled up in blankets
In a cart at the rear of his shed.

The following morn, Jonah took off at dawn
For Merthyr town, where he'd coin it, no worry.
Whale meat, up there, would go down a treat
Washed down with a bowl of hot curry.

All about town, he hawked it up and down.
At first all seemed to be going so well
But that was a very hot summer
And it very soon started to smell.

So he began hosing it down with cold water,
Jonah wanted to stop it from turning to fat
When up came a man with a large brown paper bag,
Wryly he joked, 'I'll take the lot home for our cat.'

Paddy emerged from the Old Corner House
And there he stood licking his lips,
'Well, if that's what they serve here in Georgetown
No fish pal, I'll just take the chips.'

They towed it away the very next day
As the sun was starting to rise.
It was last seen on the Old Rocky Road
Pursued by a large cloud of flies.

Death of a Song and Dance Man

Or Recalling Johnny Donovan

There's an old hearse on the Bont, he lives in the back
When he hoofs down our high street, he's out for the craic.

In his tail coat and daps, he looks gay, debonair
A down at heel version of the great Fred Astaire.

Though he's never got money, he's top of the toffs
Can sing like a linnet when he's off up the Hops.

When elections come around he'll always be found
Voting left, right and centre, and all over town.

Some days he'll go missing, and just cannot be seen
But its up to the Hops is where Johnny has been.

He can swallow an orange without peeling the skin
And stretch both of his testicles right up to his chin.

One cold winter's morning with the frost on the ground
The body of Johnny, they tell me, was found.

In a ditch by the roadside not far from the track
He went up to the Hops but he never came back.

North of the Bont where the wind razors around
The spirit of Johnny, I'm told, still is found.

Yes, the spectre of Johnny revives in the rain
As his steps rattle windows all down the Red Lane.

He tap dances his way through The Walk and Swan Street
Clad in tail coat and top hat with daps on this feet.

Underneath the streetlights when the weather gets worse
If you hold still and listen, you may hear a hearse.

And if it should pull over, it will be no sin
To tap on the window and ask, 'Is Johnny in?'

Liar Land

There is this place called Liar Land,
All silver sea and shifting sand.

Where each morning, every day
Another liar comes to stay.

On this fine morning under billowed sails
In blows King Elvis then the Prince of Wales.

That title, of itself a lie
Defending, many had to die.

In the evening you may espy
That cad Lord Lucan passing by.

And Lucky Lucan boasts a horse
Its name is Shergar, well of course.

Each one has stories he can tell
Of how his life's not going well.

How he spent a fortune on a boat
Just to find the bloody thing won't float.

We watch them come, we watch them go
Where they wind up, we'll never know.

One thing for sure we know as they march passed
Like time, this Liar Land will last and last.

They come, they go
They're passing through
Not always knowing
What is what and who is who.
It's good to watch but never true
It's Liar Land.

What lies ahead?

All round the world children starve in the dust
While false politicians say that war is a must
Telling the young ones to stand up and fight
As the body count rises, there's not one in sight.

We've got the sun in the morning and the moon at night
So goes the song but, I ask you, have they got it right?
We'll not have them for long and if I'm not wrong
No high-flying birds will brighten our sky,
Fish in our rivers will be left high and dry,
Vanishing fast are our hedges and trees,
Blind men are fishing in poisonous seas.

We invest all our money on exploring the moon
Sending up rockets yet we can't fill a spoon
For the poor here on earth there's always a dearth.
For them no tomorrow, as they sit in the cold,
The unvarnished truth's that their future is sold.

What of those heartfelt promises of a brave new land
Employment, no recession, bankers bonuses banned?
And if by some chance it should all blow away
And if back we should come in a year and day.
Blair, Brown, Cameron, Clegg never more seen,
Odious images all, from a poor man's dream.
What if fields and rivers were living anew?
If this were no dream, what then would we do?

Elect a new leader and start a new world
With banners and rockets and diamonds and pearls
With food in our freezers and clothes on our racks.
I bet in a while that the wars would be back
To poison our children and blacken the land.
A bird in the hand we just can't understand.
The path to enlightenment waters the seed
Of our great iniquities: that insatiable
Drive for power and to greed.

The Computer

Come into my lap-top said the surfer from the sky
I can take you off to places and you never need to fly

I can whizz you through the universe whilst sitting in your
chair
With virtual reality you'll believe that you are there

You can buy most anything you want and never leave the
house
Then pay for it by credit card and just clicking with your
mouse

With cameras in mobile phones, there's no place to hide
They'll hunt you down with e-mails as through the net you
glide

It will take an hour at most to download some wicked game
Or visit a new website with a strange and trendy name

You will need to be on broadband in case someone should
phone
They can leave you a message to download when you get home

The world goes rushing by as before your desk you sit
No time for conversation, what need is there for it

On line you can do anything, even find yourself a wife
Or switch off the bloody thing and get yourself a life

A Sixties Salesman's Lament

Oh to be a salesman and drive a company car,
Smart thinking, hard drinking, doing business at the bar.

Speeding down the motorway, jacket on a hook,
Letting all the peasants feel envy as they look.

Oh to go to conferences in those fancy hotels
With all the boring bastards who don't want to go as well.

Oh to attend big meetings to improve the company graph,
The prospects are so marvellous and that's such a bloody
laugh.

Oh to be a salesman for whom the future looked so bright
For the comprehensive school kid who could not read nor
write.

Off you go to dinner with a buyer you can't stand,
Spending some-else's money, makes you feel so grand.

Oh to be a salesman, you can hardly bloody wait,
Then wake up and realise, you're already forty-eight.

'Arri the Black

'Old 'arri won't have you,' my mother used to say
But when we seen him coming we'd all run away

'Old 'arri won't hurt you,' he'd declare with a smile
But when we seen him coming we'd all run a mile

How he arrived in Merthyr, never did we know
We never seen a black man that time long ago

He had a strange look about him
He was one of a kind
Old 'arri couldn't see you
Old 'arri was blind

'Old 'arri won't hurt you', that's all that he ever said
Yet I dream still of 'arri though he's long since dead

Madam Sonia

In low cut evening gown, resplendent through the bar
Glides gay Madam Sonia, our own opera star
Makes eyes at the boys in the Greyhound Hotel
No-one takes any notice, they know him too well

This grand prima donna like a ship in full sail
His brassiere stuffed full with an old Western Mail
High heels and lip stick with a powder puff bag
Is queen of our high street, high priestess of drag

First thing each morning Sonia's out on our streets
Admiring the bums of the boys that he meets
With the powder and lipstick still on his face
But daytime in Dowlais is just not the place
To try out a new dress, it's Sonia's mistake
For young kids do rag him, call him a fake

They just won't allow him to do as he please
As he sweeps up the street with grandiose ease
He's strong as an ox but no cause for alarm
This ex-blacksmith's striker don't mean any harm
Just a gentle old giant shorn from his roots
A lost ballerina in old working boots

To sail through the bar
Bedecked in regalia
We all know what it means
To gay Madam Sonia
Our king of the queens

Love at first bite

He thought she was gorgeous even though she was fat
As she sat on the wall with her donna kebab.

It was three weeks later he saw her again
Stuffing curry and chips down Post Office Lane.

Swigging Red Bull, she seductively offered a sip.
Across the road he swaggered and instead snatched a chip.

The saga that started with love at first bite
Led soon to marriage, to her mother's delight.

Wedding reception, top class, was held at Hing Hongs
As guests hit the high notes with karaoke songs.

The honeymoon bus took them off to Porthcawl
To her mam's caravan that cost bugger all.

Then back to Merthyr to start a new life
As Mr and Mrs, husband and wife.

In no time at all several children had come
But the house was too small as they lived with her mum.

That didn't bother them,
They started going out.
Then the trouble started,
Of that there is no doubt.

Soon they'd forgotten how it all began,
He found a new girlfriend, she a new man.

With no turning back on this hazardous course
A year or two later they filed for a divorce.

Now Saturday nights are never the same,
Gone is the magic of Post Office Lane.

Their paths crossed again one Saturday night
When after the pub, they stopped for a bite.

Two lonely people stuffing their faces,
Two different lives, two different places.

As for the children, they go out every night,
Naturally dreaming of love at first bite.

The grillers in the mist

It's the weekends that you see them, stumbling home half-
pissed
Two on every corner, the grillers in the mist

Kebabs and chicken portions grasped in cardboard trays
Better to eat the cardboard and throw the rest away

Standing in the doorways full of broken glass
Shouting at each other, swearing as you pass

Fists full of greasy burgers
Mouths stuffed full of spiced up ham
Roads strewn with polystyrene
And regurgitated lamb

Next morning council cleaners
Convene upon the scene
They sweep away the worst
And clear up what they can

Next Friday the grillers are
Back to do the same again
Designer jeans and tee shirts
All dishevelled in the rain

With Beckham and Ronaldo printed across their backs
Noses full of powder, is there nothing that they lack

To take them back into the high street
Still looking for a fight
If they don't wind up in A. and E.
It wasn't a good night

Colour Sergeant Swazi

Free Wales Colour Sergeant from a far off land,
A different colour to others in his band.
Stumbling 'round the Anchor, mumbling in a daze,
Crumpled in the corner, in a drunken haze.

Free Wales Colour Sergeant, far away from home,
Wonders how he got here, how did he start to roam.
Living out a nightmare, goes from drink to drink.
What will happen to him? He doesn't dare to think.

Free Wales Colour Sergeant, got no place to go,
Found himself in Merthyr, how he'll never know.
Not for him a history, no-one knows his past,
Sleeping in a corner to make his money last.

Free Wales Colour Sergeant passed away one day
In a filthy lock-up, nothing more to say.
People ask about him, wonder where he's gone.
Tales of his sojourn here linger on and on.

Somewhere out in India, people knew him well.

Do they still remember? Impossible to tell.

Back up here in Merthyr, no-one understands

Why he chose to die here, bottle in his hands.

All for a Watch and Chain

Down he went when it was still dark
And never came up no more
She lost a husband, he a life
Then things went on as before

Take him to Cefn, carry the coffin
The coal board can never explain
Why he spent all his days down in the dark
And all for a watch and chain

From child to grandfather, father to son
Never would you hear them complain
Born to go down in the dust to their deaths
And all for a watch and chain

Values have altered as time has marched on
Now it's money we all have on the brain
No downing tools when the union so rules
But what price the watch and the chain

Where have all the good times gone?

Where have all the people gone, I knew when I was small?
Where are all the summer trips that went from Radcliffe Hall?

Barry every summer, in winter Band of Hope,
Japs and Tarzan in the wood, swinging from a rope.

Where are all the toys we had, slings and whips and tops,
We could play with in doorways of the posher shops?

ABC on Saturdays, Flash Gordon and King Kong,
'We are the boys and girls well known..' we did sing along.

And what about the carnival in Cyfarthfa Park,
The horse show, the dog show and the fireworks in the dark?

Children don't play proper games, they're all computer mad,
They exist in 'virtual' worlds; it makes me feel so sad.

Nobody stops to talk, except on mobile phones,
Texting each other like a bunch of bloody clones.

We don't seem to have the characters who used make us laugh.
Our lives revolve around plasma screens, too trivial by half.

When I walk along our High Street, it's full of charity shops,
Pound stores and kebab bars, that stink of incinerated slops.

The Castle, the Theatre Royal and the Temp were
Picture houses grand. There's no Wyndham sing-alongs
No Warrilows, no Sally Army Bands; the one
Thing that hasn't changed is the waitress in Hing Hongs.

Brothers embalmed

In the realm of secret people, no-one dare speak out
They're pledged to keep the secrets of what they're all about

A nod, a wink, a handshake is enough to let them know
You know, then off to wine and dine with Mister So and So

You have to be invited, you simply can't join in
It's not for the common folk, that would be a mortal sin

You must attend rehearsals for to learn your lines,
How to greet your brothers with all the secret signs

Then the grand Induction with others like yourself
Garb you in costume like a goblin or an elf

It's said if you betray them, they'll cut out your tongue
But that's all behind you, a new life has begun

They welcome you with open arms, hail brother and well met
As to lodge activities, it's your duty to 'forget'

Soon it's onwards and upwards, your goal to reach the top
Grand master of the local lodge, where-ever will it stop?

Dressing up for gatherings with your new found friends
Until you pass away, and that's not where it ends

And when at last you go, shake off this mortal coil,
Same place as us you'll be, beneath six feet of soil

Then when you reach the pearly gates and give the secret sign
Tough luck, just like the rest of us, you'll have to wait in line

Conversation stopper

It's a terrible world, you have to agree
With no conversation, no afternoon tea.

No place you can go to have a good chat,
Lap top computers have put paid to that.

Recall the excitement when letters would come
And you'd split them open with finger and thumb

And then in a while you would send a reply,
A means to ensure that no friendship would die.

Now in an instant the world's at your feet,
The clothes you wear and the food that you eat.

You don't have to leave the house when you want to shop
For an elegant gown or a bottle of pop.

Click on an icon, in an instant it's done
Result no more shopping, but then there's no fun.

And when you venture away from the screen
It's not the same as the place you've just been.

You can journey on Google as far as you like
But for proper time travel choose car, foot or bike.

Down for the Day

Meet at the café, can't start without food,
One in the Anchor, to get in the mood.

Off to the station with ticket and scarf,
Smash a few milk bottles just for a laugh.

Merthyr to Cardiff, our plan not to pay,
Pushing old people who get in the way.

Running like mad men to get to the pub,
Three pints of Skull Attack, now for some grub.

Flasks in our pockets, money to burn,
Hot dogs then whiskies, when will we learn.

Then down to the Arms Park, bursting to pee,
I've got a North Stand, sneak in next to me.

Insulting the linesmen, the ref' is a bum,
Accusing our pack of collapsing the scrum.

The game is over, our team has gone down
So three pints of Strongbow, then back up town.

One in the Welly, then off to Hing Hongs,
Mocking the Chinese with rude rugby songs.

Bending the cutlery, no-one will pay,
Sent for the cops but we all got away.

Home on the bus, as sick as a dog,
Spending the night asleep in the bog.

Up in the morning, a terrible head,
Just can't remember a thing that I said.

Was it all worth it? What did we do?
Where did we go, when, why and with who?

Pockets are empty and our cash down the drain,
Contents of stomachs on the floor of the train.

Tongue like a carpet, police at the door,
If I get over this, never no more.

Next time they play, I'll watch it on TV
Feel a bit better. Well, let's wait and see.

Growing nowhere fast

Sixteen soon and growing up so fast.
Nothing is forever; nothing seems to last.

Faster and faster, the world's in a spin.
Boyfriends and make-up; we can never stay in.

Twenty and thinking of just one guy.
Greece for our holidays; teens have passed us by.

Now thinking of babies and carpets instead.
Faster and faster; we can't wait to get wed.

Faster and faster; time starts to fly.
Long gone is that glint in the teenager's eye.

Thirty and thinking of what we missed,
The boys in the playground we loved and we kissed.

Striving with grace to hold back our fears
When forty and facing the oncoming years.

Wondering, is it worth holding on
When fifty and sadly the children have gone.

With time on our hands we dwell on the past.
What made us think that the magic would last?

What of the promises that once we made?
As we grow old, how they dwindle and fade.

Sixty and all is less of a rush.
We love life about us but also the hush.

While all the world is dashing about,
We are quietly pleased that we are left out.

Seventy and grey: days closing in.
Thoughts of our school days are rekindled again.

Faster and faster, should our stories be told?
Write it all down before dementia takes hold.

Faster and faster until at last we are free
To look back and say, as a child starts to play,
I remember when that child was me.

The Eagle's Last Flight

Did his eyes deceive him as it appeared above the town,
gliding?
Was this the mystical bird that once inspired the Merthyr
Rising?

On wings of green and white it circled high over Argos and
Matalan.
This emblem of our glorious past, exclaimed he, I'll follow in
my van.

His vision fleetingly obscured as across the sun it floated,
Then heavenward it soared, its plumage, as if in gilt were
coated.

Then downward dived to the river Taf, menacing and deep
Where rusting trolleys stalled the flow and clogged the salmon
leap.

Caught in the up-draught from a passing bus, it got tangled in a tree.
Abandoning his van, this bird of legend he would attempt to free.

Oh what, to Merthyr folk, would be this great eagle's message?
What new political storm did its arrival presage?

But when he got there he found it was only an empty ASDA plastic bag.

In the wake of the Aberfan Disaster

Do not look for them on glorious Spring mornings
When all of the valley is bathed in light
When the whole hillside is verdant and bright.

Come on days when rain has flattened grass to hill
And tree tops hover above the morning mist,
Life was over for them on a day such as this.

Do not seek them in the school-yard
Before the bell that tolled their doom
Recalled them to the old classroom.

You will not find them in the street
Where children meet and love to play
Or in those Summer meadows,
Haring through the breeze blown hay.

Not one to knock a door then run away
Or scrump an apple on a balmy day.

Come on a day in Autumn and walk above the town.
Stop there and listen. Can you hear the tip come down?

The cold coat of tragedy that cloaked the school after dawn
Enclosing all those children who from families were torn,
Left in its wake an emptiness, a school where nothing stirred,
A town bereft where young voices were no more to be heard.

Do not look for them in the shops, or on the bus, hair parted,
Standing in a line as was the practice when they started
School before assembly, not one is there, not one alive,
Some little solace from the awful anguish to derive.

Do not look for them as youngsters in their teens
About the town and walking in their waking dreams.

Do not look for them when they're older and it's time to wed,
No consolation there, as well you know, most all are dead.

There is a spot above the town and high upon that hill
Where grieving mothers, years later, place still a daffodil.

Take time to ponder how it might have been

Had fate that morning staid her hand or had the Coal Board
planned

To monitor the slipping land; it would have been a different
scene.

Then some other town, some other time, would have born the
brunt

Of a government indifferent. The compensation's paid

But that's as nought for children's lives and a town's soul
unmade.

A Golfer's Ascent

Eight in the morning, just picture the scene,
Mist rolling in over fairway and green.

Out of the clubhouse with trolleys and bags
Come bleary-eyed golfers, some smoking fags.

To get to the eighteenth hole will be enough
To stop them from losing their balls in the rough.

Then back to the clubhouse, to some it's a great shame
They must spend so much money on improving their game.

They'll purchase a new iron or maybe a wedge
While other poor blighters can't afford fruit and veg'.

Yes being a golfer is a wonderful life,
'Specially as it gets you away from the wife.

So when it's all over and you finally die
And they take you to play on that course in the sky

Will Gabriel be waiting to open the door?
Will he duck and shout 'Bugger' when someone shouts 'Four'?

If he let's you in, will you thank God and pray?
For playing in heaven there's no green fees to pay.

There you play all day long and even at night
With the moonshine and the stars providing the light.

It must be quite thrilling when playing off par
When you birdie a bogey right next to a star.

As back down on earth a new player is born
And you watch him practise with his dad on the lawn.

You know that one day he'll be just like you,
Playing free golf up there beside God in the blue.

The last word

I feel so sick with my dreams on tick
And everything left to pay.
My own gravy train is driving my brain,
It's ruining my life away.

Booze and baccy, wild women and song,
I'm well down the road of decay.
Live for moment, life is not long.
Yes, the devil is here to stay.

Hi there old timer
What will you do on Judgement Day?
Run like hell at the warning bell
And fall flat on your face on the way?

Then on passed the post like a drunken ghost
Not a word of rebuttal to say.
What was self-belief has now turned to grief
And you cannot recall how to pray.

Hey, your landlord loves you old timer,
He told me so just the other day.
You owe nothing to life old timer,
There's all the time in the world to pay.

Old timer, you'll remember the days
When employment was easy to find
And all our pockets were stuffed with pay.
There was no call to go on the dole,
Our tomorrows were a world away.

Old man, shall we dive straight into hell,
Get used to the smell of drunkenness
And decay, or go meekly like lambs
To our fate, then cry out for our mams
And own up to our sins on the way?

The reaper is waiting, hook in hand,
Now then, what have you got to say?
'Wail until Friday, I'll pay you then
For tomorrow's another day.'

Far away down the street the faint tramp of feet
Tells us they're trudging their way into work.
'Clowns' we do call them but in truth we're the fools
Who broke all the rules to evade irksome and
Unwelcome work that we frequently shirked to
Spend most of our time drinking whisky and wine.
Will God spare us? Unlikely, but he just may.

Look over your shoulder old timer,
The reaper is ready to pounce.
Like you old timer, I've written off debts
Built on lost bets and a lifestyle
I've failed to renounce, and when it comes
To the end, no ear will I bend.
The truth is I won't have word to say.

You and me both old timer,
Let's plead for more time on this earth
To show the world that we're worth
Saving. Oh Lord let it be true
Because time for me's tight and
I'm much older than you.

I Say

Christmas is coming, I say what a bloody fuss.
Old men sleeping in the doorway outside Toys-R-Us.

Drunken party revellers dropping in the street,
Nothing around their shoulders, nothing upon their feet.

Taxis full of shoppers, heaped with electronic games
Extolling crime and violence, yet with romantic names.

Electronic santas riding motor-bikes,
Electronic gizmos, doing anything you like.

What a merry Christmas, but we're all out of work
So it's round the next corner that poverty does lurk.

Christmas is coming and the goose is getting fat.
Soon it will be over, I say thank the Lord for that.

I Wonder

I have met dissemblers here, whose boasts outshine the sea.

I have met men of integrity, far better men than me.

I have heard the tales that men have told, of broken lives and dreams.

I have seen regimes collapse and the demise of their grand schemes.

I have suffered baleful nights and agonising days

Yet I have watched the sun come up in a thousand golden rays.

And all this for me, a simple man, is hard to understand

Why all of this great wonder is found in my own land.

And all of it for nothing, perhaps to watch and wonder at,

Perhaps to look and learn.

Expiry Date Is On The Beak

Where do pirates' parrots go to die
When they expire and topple from the sky?
As soon as their beaks start turning blue
When parakeets have had a cockatoo
Do they find it kind of hard to fly?

I rarely see them around and about
When I go shopping they are never out.
Are they on some far off isle
Seeking treasure with a smile?
Many yarns they could relate no doubt.

It must be quite frustrating in the end
When all your life you've been a pirate's' friend.
When you're becalmed upon that pirate ship
And know you're making that last ocean trip
Home, and are about to ascend
To heaven. On the other hand

Captain Flint, a parrot never bolder
Than when perched upon John Silver's shoulder,
Was it his renowned refrain 'Pieces of eight'
That consigned him to an undeserving fate
In hell where together they will smoulder?

So when you're next on holiday in Spain
And need to shelter from the rain
Join a pirates' night. It's an absolute delight
But first ensure you have the dress code right,
Don't put the horse before the cart,
Without a parrot you won't look the part.

That Old Man

When that old man sat on the bench over there
Walked down with me from the tip in our town
We talked of what it was like in his youth
When he worked underground.

'My father carried me down on his back
I could not have been more than ten
Monday to Saturday, morning to night
Then he would carry me home again.

Black as the coal he hewed I was
With my tin, my lamp and my jack
Lighting our way as best I could
From my perch on the old man's back.

Our mam was waiting
With piping hot water in a fireside tub
After my dad had finished washing
My turn it was for a good long scrub.

Dry by the fire
By the light of a lamp
And the smell of washed pit clothes
Slowly drying, warm but still damp.

Broth or potch for our dinner
Too tired to drag myself to bed
The sights and sounds of the day
Running still through my head.

At last fast to sleep
Til at the dawn the next day
It was straight back to work
With no time for play.

All my life
I scrapped a living down the pit
And what, I ask myself
Have I to show for it?

A scar on my face
A plate in my head
And of course dust on the chest
Long since, I should have been dead.

When I think of the times I lay on my back
In the dark, the wet and the cold
With no-one to talk to but the rats at my side
Never should I have lived to be this old'.

As we sit on the bench my thoughts turn back
To the time when I was a boy
Why is that I cannot remember the bad things
Only the moments of joy?

Casa Grande

A homage to a glorious eating/entertaining establishment on the Algarve

Casa Grande, where cuisine's superb and never bland
Where visitors are diverse, sometimes beyond belief
From poets, actors, rajas to an indian chief.

Casa Grande, a theatre of sort in a far off land
Where all manner of players on life's stage still engage
With the finest company there to enthral them all
Regardless of capital, colour, creed or of age.

Casa Grande's a very special place to dine,
Delectable dishes, a surfeit of wine
That draws the sharpest raconteurs. They come round
Because repartee is never found wanting,
Rhetoric never less than scintillating.

Truth to tell, there are doubters but we know full well
That Casa Grande often greet guests from Spirit Land.
The respect that they command is no more nor less
Than we would accord a king who would with a clown
Sit down, as indeed they did when circus people
Came to dine together with a three legged cat
Who became, in time, a particular friend of mine.

Come round but please don't bring your mobile phone,
Forget your laptop too, leave that at home,
Just bring your personality
Come sit, enjoy good food with me.

Pop goes a Gerald

I pass him up in Dowlais
As I travel out of town.
When I turn in by Hoovers
He's on his way back down.

He's down in Abercanaid
Then he's up in Incline Top.
It's best foot forward Gerald
Your legs they never stop.

'Tis said there's more than one
Of that there is no doubt.
In fact I dare suggest
There's scores of them about.

With so many of them
He can't be just one man
Every Gerald furnished
With his own plastic can.

I have often wondered
Where the Geralds have been.
Was it out for cider
Or just Pink Paraffin?

At the closing of each day
Their wanderings complete
Who gives them food for thought
And something nice to eat?

At night when we're all sleeping
And warmly bedded down,
Can it be some Geralds are
Still wandering around

To pick up discarded crisp packets
And empty bottles of pop?
Do they ever get frustrated
If they're left not a drop?

And spare a thought for those
The Geralds leave at home.
Who tunes in the Archers
When they decide to roam?

Who sweeps ashes off the mat
And who cleans out the grate?
Who boots out the mangy cat
When the Geralds come home late?

With so many Geralds
All wandering about
I fail to understand
Who lets them out
Which begs the bigger question
Who lets them in?

Farewell to a Friend

The times we shared on distant shores, our adventures near
and far
Will stay forever in our thoughts, they are part of what we are.

We sang, we drank, we had great times, what stories we could
tell
And with your passing on my friend, it's time to say farewell.
For life is just a whisper, like the motion of the seas
That brings times we remember on occasions such as these.

Goodbye old friend, we'll miss you, what is there left to say
Except we're glad we met you, God speed you on your way.

Dedicated to Claudia and Joshua and his lost socks

For more than twenty years, everything was working out fine
But life was about to change, big time, for PC 69.

He'd spent the last two years alone, on duty in the square
Just him, the pigeons and the tramps, but no-one seemed to care.

He planned a trip aboard his boat along with Bounce his dog
At length the trip had run its course, he'd written his last log.

Then from out the mists of Jersey, another lonely soul
Was looking for a better life, to make a half life whole.

And as in life it happens when fate decides to play her hand
To turn the tide of loneliness as the sea turns on the sand.

It was through an introduction that Claudia caught his eye
One cold November evening as fireworks lit up the sky.

As they found themselves together, sailors on life's sea,
They set sail for Avalon, where-ever that may be.

Several years later, still they sail the bay of dreams;
Sometimes they drop anchor to devise new plans and schemes.

If they could change the plans they made, would they turn back
the clock?
They'll never recover the life they left, no more than that lost
sock.

Lightning Source UK Ltd.
Milton Keynes UK
UKOW06f1448091015

260200UK00001B/6/P